Human Rights

FREEDOM OF EXPRESSION

Kaye Stearman

Wayland

Titles in the Human Rights series

Clean Environment

Food

Freedom of Expression

Homeland

Justice

Shelter

Cover illustrations: The Nazi concentration camp at Sachsenhausen, 1941; *inset* Anti-Nazi demonstration in Germany, 1992.

Typeset by Dorchester Typesetting Group Ltd
Printed and bound by G. Canale & C.S.p.A., Turin, Italy

First published in 1993 by
Wayland (Publishers) Ltd
61 Western Road, Hove
East Sussex BN3 1JD
England

© Copyright 1993 Wayland (Publishers) Ltd

Editor: Cath Senker
Designer: Joyce Chester

British Cataloguing in Publication Data
Stearman, Kaye
Freedom of Expression. – (Human Rights)
I. Title II. Series
323.44

ISBN 0-7502-0833-3

Acknowledgements We would like to thank all the organizations that provided information including: Amnesty International, Article 19, Index on Censorship, International P.E.N. and Liberty, and all the individuals who assisted with advice and support, including: Paul Crook, David McDowall, Suzanne Pattle, Guy Thornton and Rachel Warner. Special thanks to Margaret Burr and other library staff at the Centre for Humanities Education, Tower Hamlets Professional Development Centre, for help with the resource list.

The last three chapters of this book contain case studies which, although based upon real situations, are fictitious.

Picture acknowledgments

The author and publishers would like to thank the following for allowing illustrations to be reproduced in this book: Camera Press (J Fields) 11, 12, 14, (P Hansen) 18, (J Furmanovsky) 23, 27, (J Fields) 36, 37 and 39; Howard J Davies 13, 24 (below); Format (M Murray) 4, (B Prince) 19, (R Kempadoo) 20, (J O'Brien) 24 (above), (M Wilson) 25, (U Preuss) 34 and 44; M Geels 30; Hutchison 5, 6, (A Hill) 29, (J Egan) 32, (R Aberman) 33; Life File (A Enock) 39; Pacemaker Press 25; Photri (M Boroff) 9; Popperfoto *cover* (background), (K Kishore) 21, 41; Rex Features *cover* (inset) and title page, 7, 10, 16, 22, 26, (E Boldizsar) 31, (Witt) 38, 42; Topham 28, 40; UNICEF (R Mera) 8.

Contents

1
Express yourself!

A STREET in the old quarter of Lhasa, the capital of Tibet. A young Tibetan girl darts towards an American tourist, presses a crumpled paper into his hand and disappears. On the paper is written in English, 'Long live free Tibet – please help us', followed by the names of three Tibetan prisoners in a Lhasa jail.

During conflicts children try to find ways to express their fear and confusion. This drawing by a Palestinian child shows aircraft bombing homes in a refugee camp.

A young Somali refugee draws pictures in a classroom in a big Canadian city. When he first arrived from Somalia he sat silent and unmoving. Now he talks a little, but spends most of his time drawing, mainly pictures of planes bombing his city and people fleeing. Sometimes this refugee draws happy scenes of his life before the fighting. He is starting to smile again and is beginning to play with the other children.

A schoolroom in England. A lively group of teenagers are discussing the next issue of their school magazine. But there is no buzz of chatter. Instead they are using their arms and hands to communicate in their own language, BSL – British Sign Language. They are some of the 50,000 deaf people in Britain who use this language.

A busy night in the streets of Recife, a big Brazilian city. Two young girls sit in the shadows, talking nervously to an adult. They are street children, without families or permanent homes, and they fear the police will arrest them. They are giving their details to the adult, who works for an organization which assists street children. They hope that she can help them to get identity documents, which will make their lives safer.

In a classroom in Alaska an Inuit (Eskimo) school student taps a message into a computer. He is sending a

Deaf people often face discrimination in employment because hearing people assume that they cannot communicate. This young deaf man is learning interview skills through sign language.

letter by electronic mail to friends he has never met at a suburban high school in Sydney, Australia. They are all part of a world-wide schools computer network.

Another night, another classroom, this time in the province of Kosovo in the former Yugoslavia. This is not a regular school. Like most people in Kosovo, the students speak Albanian, but the government has banned all education in Albanian so the students must study secretly. They are quiet and attentive because they know if the police find them, they will be beaten and arrested.

Poor children in a slum in Rio de Janeiro, Brazil. It is hard for children like these to speak out for their rights.

What do all these young people, from different areas of the world and with different problems, have in common with each other? There is one common link. Sometimes slowly and sometimes painfully, they are trying to communicate with others, to express their needs and feelings on subjects which are important – often vital – to themselves. By doing so they are exercising one of the most deeply-felt human rights – the right to freedom of expression.

In almost every society people have some rights to speak freely. Often these rights are limited to a particular time and place or to a certain group, and other groups are excluded. For example, in ancient Greece all adult citizens were allowed to air their views freely and to criticize the city government – but women and slaves were not counted as citizens.

It wasn't until the French and American revolutions in the eighteenth century that the right to free expression became part of any country's legal system. One famous law is the First Amendment of the US Bill of Rights. Written in 1789, it states, in part: 'Congress . . . should not restrict freedom of speech, the press or right of people to assemble peaceably and to ask the government to put right their grievances.' Today, over two hundred years later, this statement is still regarded as the legal basis of freedom of expression in the USA.

In 1948, when the first members of the newly-formed United Nations (UN) agreed on the text of the Universal Declaration of Human Rights, they included the right to speak freely as a basic human right. Article 19 of the Declaration states: 'Everyone has the right to freedom of opinion and expression; this right includes freedom

A painting of the French Revolution of 1789, which was an important landmark for the right to free expression.

to hold opinions without interference and to seek, receive and impart information and ideas through any media and regardless of frontiers.'

The Declaration in itself is not binding on the countries that sign it (i.e., legally, they do not have to follow these standards) but if they sign it, they are sending a message to the world that they want to try to live up to these standards. Many countries have also signed the International Covenant on Civil and Political Rights of 1966, which includes the right to freedom of opinion and expression.

Many adults think of freedom of expression as being a right which only adults can use and enjoy. They may say that children are too small to understand, or that adults should speak on their behalf. But Article 13 of the United Nations Convention on the Rights of the Child, adopted by the UN in 1989, clearly states that this right also belongs to children.

Put in simple language, the Convention says that all children have the right to seek, receive and give all kinds of information and ideas in speech, writing, publishing, art or any other way they choose. This applies inside a country and across international borders. Although they may not realize it, all the young people at the beginning of this chapter are making use of these rights.

Children from around the world were brought to the UN in November 1989 to celebrate the adoption of the UN Convention on the Rights of the Child.

Yet fine words and good rules do not in themselves ensure that human rights are observed by governments. In many countries individuals who express unusual or unpopular views are treated as mad or criminal. Sometimes governments deny whole peoples freedom of expression by censoring books, banning meetings and demonstrations, and refusing people the right to found and join political parties, trade unions, or other organizations.

It is easy to assume that countries with elected democratic governments will ensure our right to speak freely. But this freedom only exists if we, as individuals, care about it and act to protect it. As with other rights, having freedom of expression involves duties and responsibilities. We need to be prepared to present alternative views and be ready to listen critically to all sides, even when we do not agree with some of them. Also, freedom of expression should not mean freedom to use deliberate lies. Nor should it be used to spread hatred or to encourage violence.

This book gives examples from many countries to show how brave and determined people, including children, use words and images to break down barriers of prejudice, poverty and violence, to achieve rights for themselves and for others.

2
Speaking up

W E ALL disagree with our governments at some stage in our lives. Perhaps we do not like a new law or we feel that politicians are corrupt or stupid. We might express our views in our schools or workplaces, in newspapers or on television, through a political party or by demonstrating on the streets. In a democracy, the right to question the government is accepted as normal. Of course, governments also have the right to reply to criticism. If we are fair-minded we will listen to all the different arguments and make up our own minds about an issue.

American anti-war protesters using their right to demonstrate. They are protesting against their government's involvement in the 1991 Gulf War against Iraq.

But what if a government will not accept the right of the people to criticize? Instead it punishes its critics. It might bully them or spread lies about them, arrest, imprison or even kill them. This not only punishes critics but also frightens other people who might have been critical. You would have to be very brave or very foolish to openly question the government in such circumstances.

Government laws alone cannot ensure freedom of expression. Other kinds of protection are needed. One of these is an independent legal system. If a government tries to limit an individual's freedom of expression, then the proper role of the legal system is to uphold the right of the individual against the government. However, this can be a long, complicated and expensive process.

It is important that individuals know their rights. Informed and active people are much less likely to accept restrictions on their speech, writing or other activities than those who are ignorant. So an education system that encourages people to think clearly and critically is vital.

Most Burmese worship in a Buddhist temple like this one. Buddhism is a peaceful religion, but the Burmese Government has used widespread violence against its people.

It is often said that a 'free press' is one of the most important ways of protecting freedom of expression. A 'free press' means that the media – not just newspapers and magazines, but also radio, television and cinema – are free from government restrictions or interference. If the media want to criticize the government, political parties or any other aspect of life, they can do so without fear of being punished. Yet, as we shall see in the next chapter, there are some restrictions on press freedom in every country.

When freedom of expression is not allowed in a country, it usually means that there is a lack of other human rights. A government that does not allow the people to discuss its business probably has shameful acts to hide. That is why some people say that freedom of expression is the most important single human right, because without it, no other demands could ever be expressed.

One country that has shown no regard for basic human rights is Burma (also called Myanmar), in south-east Asia. Very few outsiders, such as journalists or tourists, are able to visit Burma, and information about the country can be difficult to obtain. However, we do know that thousands of people have been arrested, tortured and deliberately killed by the Burmese Government.

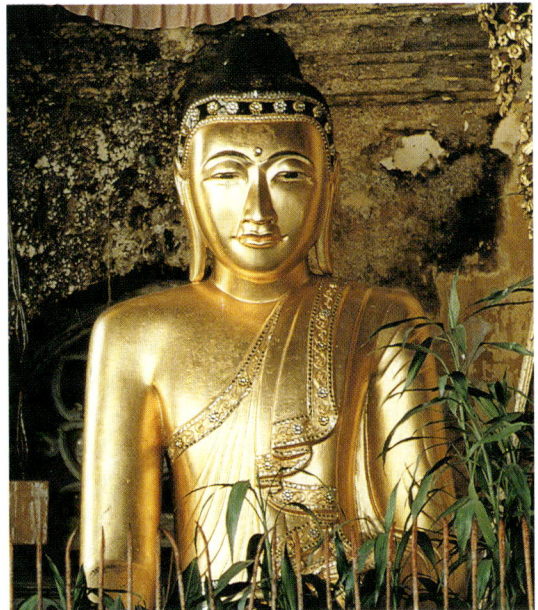

Beautiful gold objects like this giant Buddha may make Burma look wealthy but most people there are very poor.

Burma has thousands of political prisoners. Nearly all of them are in jail because they tried to exercise their basic human right of freedom of opinion and expression. Although they were critics of the military government, very few had used violence. Most had participated in peaceful demonstrations, calling for democratic change. It was mainly the government that had used violence. In September 1988, when university students demonstrated in the capital, Rangoon, government troops used tanks and guns, killing about 3,000 people. The army has also killed many thousands of peasants in the countryside.

In 1989 the government declared that there would be free elections in 1990. Perhaps even the military government had been so shocked by the demonstrations that it decided that some changes were needed. It was the first time that the people of Burma had ever had a chance to elect their own government.

In February 1990 Win Thein was a fourteen-year-old student at a junior high school in North Okkalapa, Rangoon. Like many other Burmese he was swept up in the excitement about the elections. He was too young to vote but he knew that he disagreed with the military government and he wanted to express his opinion. Together with his friends, Kyaw Soe Lwin and Thein Tun U, Win Thein put up anti-government posters on the school walls.

The three boys were immediately arrested. We don't know what happened next but they were probably badly beaten up while being questioned. They were all sentenced by a military tribunal in April 1990 to thirteen years' imprisonment under a law that said they were 'destructive elements'. There was no trial. The fact that they were only fourteen years old and should have had special protection made no difference. Win Thein and his friends are serving their prison sentences in Insein Prison, Rangoon.

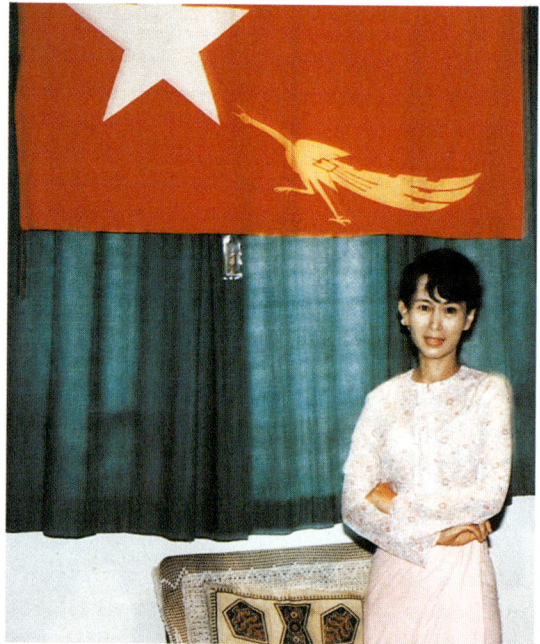

Aung San Suu Kyi, who has been under house arrest since 1989.

The most famous prisoner in Burma is Aung San Suu Kyi, the leader of the National League for Democracy. In the elections of May 1990 the National League for Democracy won about 80 per cent of the votes. In a democratic country the party would have formed a government. In Burma thousands of its supporters were imprisoned. Some were later released. The government says Aung San Suu Kyi will also be released if she gives up her support for democracy and for her party. But she refuses to do so. In 1991 she was awarded the Nobel Peace Prize for her 'non-violent struggle for democracy and human rights'.

The Burmese Government has restricted freedom of expression in other ways. At the beginning of 1991, people who worked for the government were required to answer questions on their political views and whether they had participated in anti-government demonstrations. By October that year over 15,000 of them had been sacked. Those who remained were banned from participating in any political activities. They were told that the ban also applied to their families.

As many of those who had taken part in the 1988 demonstrations were students, one of the first steps the government took was to close the secondary schools and universities. They stayed closed for three years and even after some were reopened during 1991 they remained under strict military supervision. Hundreds of teachers and university lecturers lost their jobs.

Today, troops and armoured personnel carriers patrol the streets all around Rangoon. Every public building has troops nearby. Gatherings of more than four people are banned, so meetings and demonstrations are not possible. If a person needs to travel from one town to another, he or she must first report to the military authorities. All the media remain under the control of the government.

Very few countries have such a dreadful human rights record as Burma, but it is easy to assume that what has occurred there could only happen far away. Unless the right to freedom of expression is protected, by our government, our legal system, our media and, most of all, by us as individuals, then it could happen to us.

Many thousands of Burmese have fled to neighbouring countries as refugees. In May 1992 these Rohingya Muslims were living in a refugee camp in Bangladesh.

3
Writing rights

Many governments ban or censor books and magazines. They give various reasons for their actions. For example, they may say that a particular piece of work is unpatriotic or dangerous to national security, that it makes fun of a leader or a main political party, that is too religious (or not religious enough), or that it is too experimental and hard to understand.

Andrei Sinyavsky, a Russian writer who was sentenced to seven years' imprisonment in 1965 for publishing 'anti-Soviet' works.

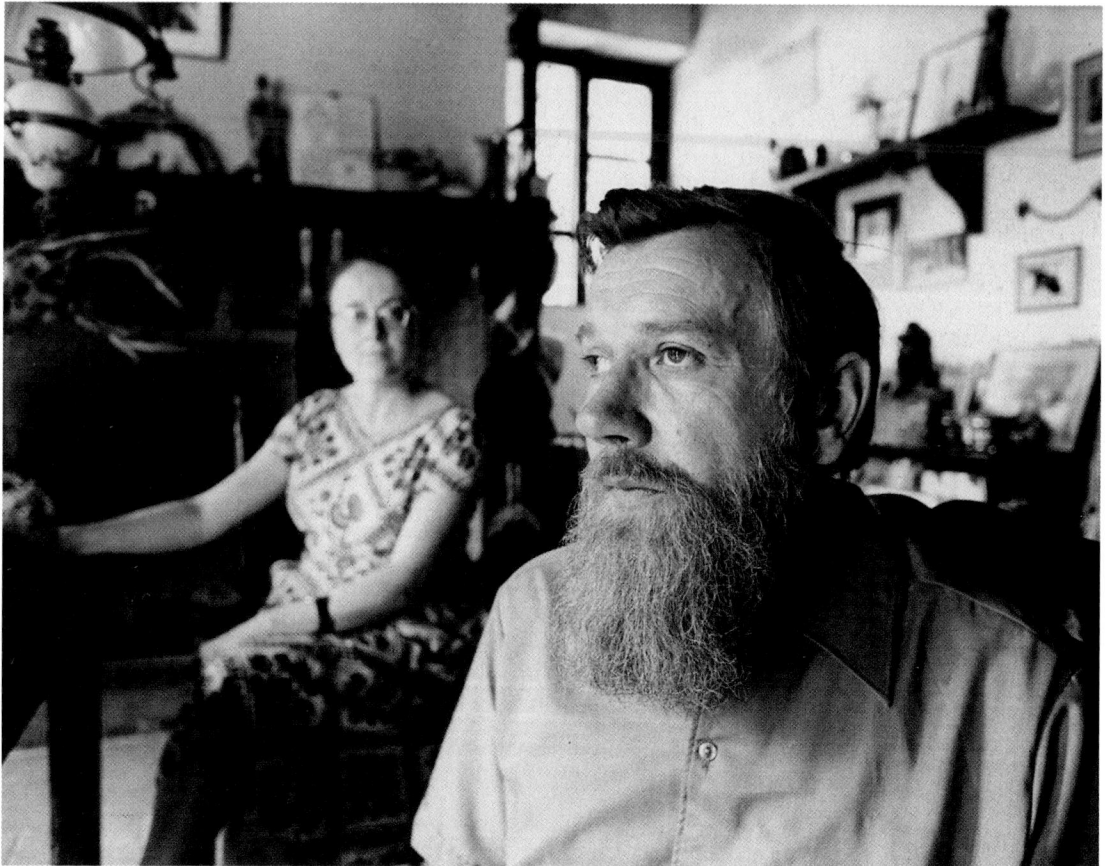

Under the Communist system in the former USSR, many foreign books and magazines were banned. The government owned the publishing firms and writers were only permitted to publish work approved by the government. The Communist Party said that literature should give a positive view of life under Communism and not show its negative features. Approved writers were rewarded with prizes and special privileges. Writers whose work was banned were arrested or exiled. Some spent many years in prison in harsh conditions.

However, banned writers found ways to produce their work. Handwritten or typed manuscripts, called *samizdat* (self-published), were secretly circulated. Some writers managed to have their work published abroad and copies were later smuggled into the Soviet Union.

From the mid-1980s, government controls on literature were loosened. Most imprisoned writers were released while others returned from exile. Many previously banned works were published. By the time the Communist system collapsed in 1991, there was widespread freedom of expression in the Russian republic.

These young Russians are showing their interest in new books at the Moscow Book Fair, 1989.

Yet writers faced new problems. It became more and more difficult to find publishers willing to consider work which was experimental or unusual. Under the new economic system, publishing firms only wanted to publish material they considered profitable. With unemployment growing, most Russians could no longer afford to buy books. Even paper for books was in short supply. Today, writers in Russia are in the same position as writers in many other countries; they can express themselves freely, but their books might not be published.

In many countries some individuals or groups are still denied the right to write and publish freely. Some of these are Communist countries, such as China and Cuba. But most are not Communist, and some are very anti-Communist. The link between all these countries is that the government wants to control the thinkers and writers in order to keep control over the rest of the population.

This may seem to be rather strange. After all, not everybody has the time to read books or is interested in reading, especially if the book is an unusual or difficult one. Not everyone can afford to buy books. In many countries, large numbers of people cannot read, and in others, there are so many books available that no one would ever have time to read them all.

A scene from the television series of Roots, *based on the book by Alex Haley. The series, which told the often hidden story of slavery and discrimination faced by black Americans, reached a wide audience in the USA.*

Although they may only reach a relatively small number of people, governments may see books as dangerous, since they can give people new ideas and encourage them to rethink their pasts and look forward to new futures.

Sometimes books make a huge impact. In nineteenth-century America, *Uncle Tom's Cabin*, a novel by a white woman, Harriet Beecher Stowe, described the horrors of slavery for black Americans. In the twentieth century, a descendant of an African slave, Alex Haley, wrote a novel called *Roots*. It traced the story of his family, from when it was forced from its home in Africa into slavery in America, through to the present day. Both books were best sellers in the USA and in other countries, and they helped to shape how Americans thought about slavery and its consequences.

One recent book which has influenced the way many people think about human rights is an autobiography called '*I . . . Rigoberta Menchu*': *An Indian Woman in Guatemala*. Rigoberta Menchu is a Mayan Indian, one of the indigenous people of Guatemala, a mountainous country in Central America. Human rights groups estimate that over 100,000 Guatemalans, mainly Mayans, were killed by the Guatemalan army in the 1980s. More than 400 Indian highland villages were destroyed. People who tried to organize peacefully in trade unions or who criticized the government were threatened, killed or 'disappeared' (taken away by the army never to be seen again).

Rigoberta Menchu shared this experience of death and abuse. From the age of eight she worked in the fields in order to survive. Her father, brother and mother were tortured and killed by the Guatemalan army, and, in 1980, she was forced to flee to neighbouring Mexico. Rigoberta Menchu became determined to tell the world what was happening in Guatemala.

As a young girl, Rigoberta had accompanied her father when he went from village to village, organizing trade unions for the Mayan farmers. Although she could not read, she memorized stories from the Old Testament and she told them to the villagers to inspire them to defend their land. Like most Mayans, Rigoberta and her father spoke only their own language, Quiché. Rigoberta realized that she needed to learn Spanish, since Spanish was the official language of Guatemala.

It was when she was living in exile that Rigoberta began work on her autobiography, telling her story, simply and strongly, into a cassette recorder. Her words were written on to paper by a friend from Venezuela. It took a long time and a lot of effort to make sure that everything was correct. The book was first published in Spanish in Barcelona, Spain, in 1984. Rigoberta would not have been allowed to publish it in Guatemala. Later, the book was translated into many other languages. By 1993 the English translation of the book had been reprinted eleven times. All around the world hundreds of thousands of people read her story.

Rigoberta Menchu at the presentation of her Nobel Peace Prize in Norway, December 1992. The leaders of the Guatemalan Government refused to attend the ceremony.

Few Mayan Indians were able to read Rigoberta's book, but they heard of the impact it had made outside Guatemala. In exile, Rigoberta Menchu spoke on behalf of the Maya of Guatemala, who were denied the right to speak out in their own country. She travelled the world giving lectures and she spoke at the United Nations for peace and justice in Guatemala. In 1992, at the age of only thirty-three, she was awarded the Nobel Peace Prize and was able to return briefly to Guatemala. Thousands of people turned out to greet her.

'I . . . Rigoberta Menchu' is an important book for several reasons. It is one of the few personal accounts of Indian life in Central America. It is the story of an extraordinary woman and of a whole people. And it brought world attention to human rights in Guatemala. When the Nobel Peace Prize was announced Rigoberta Menchu said: 'We have suffered from silence all these years. Guatemala has almost never been condemned for its massive human rights abuse in any international forum . . . This is a chance to make the repression public.'

4
Reporting the news

News is all around us. It appears before us daily on television and in newspapers. The development of a world-wide communications network via satellite means that we can watch events on our television screens almost as they happen, even though they may take place thousands of kilometres away in other continents.

We all have some experience of reporting news, even if we don't think of it as 'news'. When you tell your family or friends what happened at school, on the football field, or at a club, you act as an informal reporter of news. You might also have reported news in a more formal way – perhaps you have written for a school magazine, helped to make a family video, or described an incident to the police. Of course, some events might be more interesting or important to one group of people than to another, so you would use different versions of the news for different groups of people. You might try to be entertaining in your video and serious for the police.

Reporting the news raises many difficult questions. What is truth? Can there be more than one version of the truth? Can we ever find and report the whole truth or will some things always remain hidden? We may feel that we want to report only the facts about a situation, but is it really possible to find out all the facts and, if it is, how do we decide which are the most important facts?

Video technology opens the world of the moving image to everyone. This girl is learning to use video equipment.

A radio presenter for local radio, which is especially important because it covers stories of local interest not covered by the national press or television.

Imagine that you are reviewing a controversial television documentary. You probably consider yourself to be fair and unbiased, but the way you look at the film will be coloured by your previous experiences and personal beliefs. Perhaps you feel very strongly that the documentary is unfair or inadequate. But if you only give your own opinion without saying anything about the film itself, that would be unfair to your viewers. So you might start by outlining the different viewpoints expressed in the documentary and then give your personal views.

We should consider the question of bias every time we read a newspaper, listen to the radio or watch television. We should never accept that everything we read, hear or see is completely truthful and absolutely fair.

We must also make sure that we are fair-minded. Sometimes we may not want to believe what is reported because it is inconvenient or hurtful.

But if we care about the right to freedom of expression we have to face up to the problems and responsibilities involved in trying to report news in a fair and unbiased way.

Reporting the news can affect the lives of ordinary people. For example, if an aircraft crashes, is it fair or necessary to show dead bodies or grief-stricken families? How do we balance a right to free expression with a right to privacy? If we feel that our views have been inaccurately reported or our privacy has been invaded what can we do about it?

Some say that the government should pass laws to protect people's right to privacy. Yet won't these laws stop the media from doing their job of reporting the news? Is it right to restrict the media like this?

As we saw in the previous chapter, having a 'free press' means that the media are able to report on events without government restrictions or interference, or the threat of punishment. But, in practice, the issue is more complex. When a country is at war the government places restrictions on freedom of expression. It may say that this is necessary for 'national security', to keep vital information from the enemy and to stop enemy propaganda.

For the media, reporting the news during conflicts is particularly difficult.

Governments sometimes try to place restrictions on journalists. In 1988 these journalists demonstrated against the Indian Government when it tried to introduce a law designed to punish journalists for investigating government corruption.

Not only are there restrictions by governments and military authorities but reporters may be in danger from guns and bombs. Although there are international rules, which state that journalists should be able to work in safety without pressure or harassment, these rules are often ignored. The International Federation of Journalists recorded that at least sixty journalists died or were murdered while reporting conflicts in 1992, mainly in the former Yugoslavia and in Turkey.

Northern Ireland is a place where freedom of expression has been restricted because of conflict. There has been political and religious conflict in that area since the sixteenth century, when Protestant English and Scottish settlers began to take over the lands of the Catholic Irish. Most of Ireland became an independent republic in 1921 after a bitter civil war, but the north-eastern area, where most Protestants lived, remained part of the UK.

Catholics in Northern Ireland demonstrating for civil rights in 1968.

Although they were UK citizens, the Catholic minority in the north suffered discrimination in jobs and housing. In 1968 Catholics began to demonstrate for equal rights. Their peaceful demonstrations were attacked by the mainly Protestant police, so the British Army was called in to keep order. Some groups formed their own secret armies, called paramilitaries.

Between 1968 and 1992, over 3,000 people were killed in Northern Ireland, by the paramilitaries of extreme Protestants (called Loyalists) and Catholics (called Republicans), the British Army and the police. Most

people, both Protestant and Catholic, would like to find a peaceful solution but it is difficult while the violence continues, and because there are so many causes of disagreement.

During conflicts it is especially important for journalists to remain objective and to listen to different viewpoints. But this can be dangerous. If one side does not like a news report, the journalist who wrote it may be banned, restricted or punished – sometimes even killed. In Northern Ireland people are required by law to give the police any information that might prevent violent acts or which could be used as evidence in court. As a result

Protestants in the Orange Order, which is called after the Dutch prince, William of Orange, who defeated the Catholics at the Battle of the Boyne in 1688.

reporters may be threatened because some people see them as police agents.

It is not only journalists who are in danger. The *Sunday World* newspaper in Belfast has received threats from both Loyalist and Republican paramilitaries. In October 1992 a Loyalist group planted a bomb at its headquarters and issued death threats against those working on the *Sunday World*. Several newsagents refused to sell the paper because of these threats.

It is not just the secret armies that try to stop the reporting of independent information from Northern Ireland. In 1988 the British Government announced that it would not allow radio or television in Britain (including Northern Ireland) to broadcast the words of any person belonging to one of eleven listed 'terrorist' organizations in Northern Ireland. An interview with such a person could not be directly broadcast. Instead, his or her words had to be read out by an actor.

One of these listed groups was Sinn Fein, a legal, Republican political party, which participates in elections.

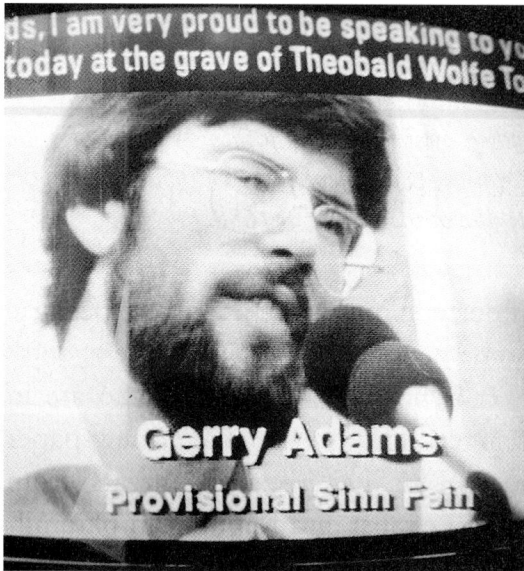

Gerry Adams, the leader of Sinn Fein, appearing on British television. His words may not be broadcast because of the ban imposed by the British Government, so they appear as subtitles instead.

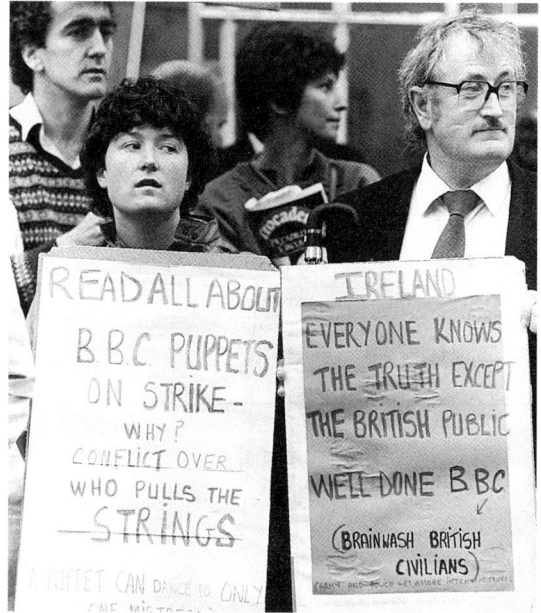

Demonstrators in 1985 protesting against the refusal of the British government-owned TV network to broadcast a controversial documentary on Northern Ireland.

Critics say that because Sinn Fein cannot present its case equally with other legal political parties, this is a denial of the party's right to freedom of expression. For the British public, it is also a denial of the right to freely receive information.

Journalists have faced another problem in Northern Ireland. A general rule of journalism is the right to keep sources of information secret, because otherwise the people who have given information might find themselves in danger. This rule is especially important when journalists are reporting in a situation of conflict and fear.

In 1991, Channel Four, a British television station, made a controversial documentary on Northern Ireland, which claimed that the Northern Ireland police force and Loyalist paramilitary groups were working together to kill Republicans. While it was being made, the television crew received death threats. The film was broadcast in October 1991.

In April 1992 the British Government charged Channel Four under the Prevention of Terrorism Act. The government said that by refusing to disclose the sources of its information Channel Four was supporting terrorists. Channel Four denied this and said that if it named its sources it would be placing others in danger. The television station said that it was investigating an important issue of corruption and security and that it was its duty to bring this information to the public. Despite protests, Channel Four was fined £75,000.

Reporting the facts in times of conflict is hard and often painful. But the pain will not disappear by restricting information and the conflicts will not end if we just ignore them.

The findings of the Opsahl Commission, which looked at peace prospects in Northern Ireland, are announced, June 1993.

5
Informing the public

Having a free media is only one step towards informing the public. Newspapers, magazines, even television and radio, may not reach everyone. They may print and broadcast freely but the information they give may be biased and incorrect. Also, editors and programme-makers need to create lively journalism and popular programmes, so that advertisers will want to advertise with them. The result is that serious issues are sometimes ignored, or screened at times when few people are watching.

If there is a crisis in a country, but the media are not allowed to report what is happening, it is difficult for people to know how to respond to the crisis. Without an informed public, governments can cover up their mistakes. An informed public places pressure on a government to act. Many governments fear that an informed public is a critical public that can threaten their power. Few governments are willing to admit their mistakes or to change their policies to prevent future mistakes.

During the Romanian Revolution in 1989 demonstrators pulled down this statue of Lenin because it was a symbol of the old government.

One government that for years denied its people basic human rights was Romania. For most of the twentieth century, Romania has been ruled by undemocratic governments. From 1965 to the end of 1989, Romania was under the dictatorship of the Communist Party leader, Nicolae Ceausescu. Those who opposed him were killed or imprisoned. People lived in fear of his secret police, the *Securitate*, too afraid to speak against the government, even to their family or neighbours. Few foreigners were allowed to visit Romania or to talk to ordinary Romanians.

Ceausescu claimed that Romania was a rich and prosperous country, thanks to the policies of his government. He controlled the media, so this lie was not challenged in the press. Romanians could see that their food and housing were actually becoming worse, but they did not dare criticize the government. As there was so little contact with the outside world they could not compare their situation with that of people in other countries.

Romanians protesting against the Communist government in December 1989.

A Romanian orphan in a children's home before the revolution. In 1992 there were still 98,000 children in Romanian orphanages.

In the late 1980s political upheavals were sweeping across Eastern Europe. By the end of 1989, popular protests had led to the overthrow of undemocratic Communist governments in Poland, Hungary, East Germany, Bulgaria and Czechoslovakia. In Romania people came on to the streets to demonstrate peacefully but the government responded with violence. After days of fierce fighting Ceausescu was overthrown and executed. The Romanian people celebrated; they thought that a new government would bring them human rights.

Yet the Romanians' problems have not ended. The poverty and disease which were created by the Ceausescu government remained. The new government was unable to bring democracy or reform by itself, and the habits of years of dictatorship could not be broken overnight.

Ceausescu had ordered that all Romanian women should have as many children as they were able to, whatever the wishes of the individual woman and her family. Consequently, there were many unwanted children. Some of these children, especially those who were sick or disabled, were placed in state orphanages. The orphanages were dirty and overcrowded, and there was little money for medicines. Diseases spread rapidly in this environment, in particular a deadly new disease called 'Acquired Immune Deficiency Syndrome', shortened to Aids.

As yet, no one knows the origins of Aids or how to cure it. We do know that Aids develops from an infection known as HIV (Human Immunodeficiency Virus). A person who is 'HIV positive' (that is, infected with HIV) will eventually develop Aids, although this may take months or years. When a person has 'full-blown' Aids, all the protective systems in their body break down. They cannot fight even small infections and they become weaker and weaker. Some people live longer than others, but no one survives the disease.

The virus that causes Aids lives in the body fluids – especially blood and semen – of an infected person. It can be passed to another person through infected blood and semen. If a person has cuts or sores the virus can enter the bloodstream more easily. The most common ways this happens is by unsafe (i.e., unprotected) sexual behaviour, by contaminated blood (used in blood transfusions), and through people sharing needles and unsterilized medical equipment. This last way appears to have been the main route of infection in the dirty conditions of Romanian orphanages.

The existence of the infected children only became publicly known after Ceausescu was overthrown. Many people inside and outside Romania were so horrified that they decided that Romanians had to be informed of the risks and course of the disease, and told how to care for those who had already been infected.

Two of these campaigners are Bogdan Enache and Dan Dumitrescu, who are chemistry students in

Aids is a major threat to millions in many parts of the developing world. Some countries, like Zimbabwe, have recognized the problem and are trying to teach people how to avoid becoming infected.

Bucharest, the Romanian capital. Dan says: 'Officially in 1990 Romania had around 1,000 Aids patients. Two years later there are 70 per cent more and that doesn't include the HIV positives. Half of all the European children who have Aids live in Romania. We have to campaign.'

Bogdan Enache and Dan Dumitrescu, Romanian students who broadcast a weekly radio programme that mixes information about Aids with pop music.

At first Bogdan and Dan became volunteers with the Red Cross, an organization which works closely with the government. As they were young themselves, they felt that it was especially important to reach other young people. They put forward many ideas for campaigns to interest them but these new approaches were ignored or rejected. Even though Ceausescu had gone, many of the old ways of thinking remained. Bogdan and Dan became more and more frustrated.

Together with about twenty others, Bogdan and Dan decided to found their own organization, ARAS – the Romanian Anti-Aids Association. Some foreign organizations helped them with finance and materials. A French-owned Romanian radio station, Fun Radio, allowed them to broadcast every Tuesday on the subject of Aids. The level of ignorance was so great that hundreds of people, young and old, contacted ARAS asking for advice and information. ARAS also runs programmes for secondary schools and universities to educate students about all aspects of the disease. By 1992 ARAS had about forty members, most of them under the age of twenty-five.

ARAS still faces many problems. It bravely says that there should be no hatred of Aids victims but most Romanians remain both ignorant and prejudiced against them. Since homosexuality is illegal in Romania and the law punishes gays with up to seven years in jail, it is extremely difficult to even mention links between unsafe kinds of homosexual activity and Aids. Many people find it difficult to talk openly about sex. Romania itself is not yet a democratic society and most of the press and television stations remain under the control of the government. But Bogdan and Dan know that unless ARAS continues with its work of educating the public then the situation can only worsen.

6
Making music

There are many ways in which people can express themselves – not just by speaking and writing but also through music, dance, painting, sculpture, video – and all other forms of artistic activity. Music, especially singing, is used by people all over the world to communicate their thoughts and feelings.

In its simplest form a song is a way in which an individual can express joy, grief, anger or despair. The song might reach a wider audience, becoming part of a family or village tradition, or even capturing the hearts and imaginations of people in towns, cities and countries far away.

Before this century, the most common way people learnt songs was from wandering musicians who travelled from village to village. Today, most parts of the world are linked through radio and television, so music can rapidly reach millions of people.

Sometimes songs are used in protest. You might not realize it, but the nursery rhyme, 'Baa, baa black sheep . . .', was a protest song against the unjust government in eighteenth-

Every community produces its own music. These musicians in Pakistan are playing traditional instruments at a reception for foreign guests.

century France. The words sound like nonsense, but they have a hidden meaning. The 'black sheep' was France, the 'master' was the king, the 'dame' was the church and the 'little boy' was the poor peasant.

Schoolgirls in Turkey. The government keeps tight control of teaching materials in Turkish schools. Teachers are given lists of books which they are forbidden to use in class.

In some countries today the government tries to control the music people create because it sees that music as a threat to its power. When a government does this, it is as much a violation of freedom of expression as when it bans books or newspapers.

The Turkish Government has been especially harsh in trying to control people's words, thoughts and music, especially those of the Kurds. Turkey is a large country lying between southeast Europe and the Middle East. Most of its 57 million citizens are ethnic Turks who speak Turkish. However, almost one citizen out of five is Kurdish. Kurds speak a different language and have a different culture and identity from Turks. Although Kurds are Turkish citizens, in practice they do not have equal rights with other Turkish citizens. Many Kurds have protested against this treatment.

During most of the twentieth century Turkey has been ruled by dictators or by the army. Even when there is an elected government the army keeps a lot of power for itself. Many basic human rights are denied to Turkish citizens. Hundreds of thousands of people, including Kurds, have been jailed and tortured for belonging to trade unions or for criticizing the government.

Asef tells his story. 'I come from a village in Malatya province, in southeastern Turkey. Everyone there was Kurdish, and we all spoke our own language. When government officials came the village elders used to speak to them in Turkish, because the law said that there was only one language in Turkey, and that was Turkish.

'When I was eight we moved to the city of Marash and I began to attend school regularly. All my schooling was in Turkish because that was the official language. At first I sat in class not understanding anything – now I speak Turkish quite well. But it's very confusing because at home we speak only Kurdish and although I can read Turkish, I can't read my own language. In any case what would I read? For years it was illegal in Turkey to publish books in Kurdish.

'Music and song are very important in my family. We are Alevis, which means "followers of Ali" and we say that we are true Muslims. We believe that it is the purity of the heart and the mind which is pleasing to God, not the outward things like fancy buildings or elaborate ceremonies. So we don't have mosques in our villages or pray five times a day. Other Muslims say that this makes us unbelievers and they call us names and sometimes beat us. So we have to be careful.

A traditional Kurdish ceremony which takes place before a wedding.

'We believe in celebrating our Alevi heritage in songs and poetry. Many of our songs are from Pir [Saint] Sultan Abdal, who in the old days died at the hands of the sultans. He said that poor people must have justice and that is still true today. Music and song have been part of our life and religion for hundreds of years.

'Like the Kurdish language, Kurdish music was also banned. We have had to sing and play in the privacy of our homes and remain very watchful. Friends and family like to come and hear us but we can't have too many people visiting or the city authorities would become suspicious. Anyway, in a small house in the city there simply isn't room. We have some cassettes of Kurdish music recorded in Germany, but we must be careful to hide them well, otherwise we could be harassed. We would like to record our own music but it's not possible.'

The laws in Turkey that restrict freedom of expression have been criticized by many other governments. They point out that Turkey has signed international conventions which are supposed to guarantee human rights there. Press censorship and intimidation are increasing and many journalists have been punished for reporting on the situation in the Kurdish areas. At least ten journalists were killed in Turkey in 1992.

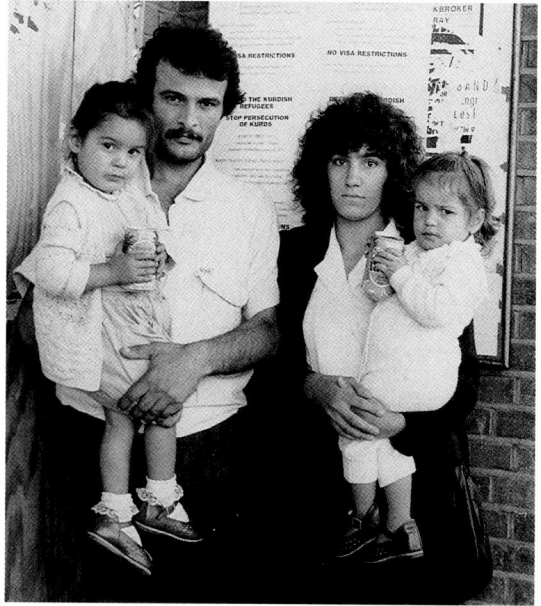

Thousands of Kurds from Turkey, especially Alevi Kurds, have fled to other European countries to escape government persecution. This Kurdish family now lives in England.

The Turkish Government has made some changes. In April 1991 the law which made the Kurdish language illegal was repealed. However, only Turkish is allowed for official use (such as for government documents and in courts). By 1992 the government had permitted the publication of a few Kurdish books and magazines, but some had to close because the publishers were harassed. In many areas there are still restrictions on Kurdish music and dance being performed in public. For Asef and his family, Kurdish music is still a secret and private pleasure, always shadowed by fear.

7
Language and mother tongue

'When I was at school everything was taught in French. It was bizarre. I was a Melanesian living in the tropics in the Pacific, yet at school I was learning about trains, snow and the history of France.'

These are the words of Nicole, a young Kanak woman from New Caledonia – which she prefers to call Kanaky – a group of islands lying between Australia and New Zealand.

Her situation may seem unusual, but many other peoples have similar experiences. The right to speak and to be educated in your own language (called 'mother tongue') and to know your own culture and history, seems such a basic one that most people take it for granted.

These kindergarten children in Wales are starting to learn Welsh, their mother tongue.

Yet, in many countries children are denied this right. Kurds in Turkey are educated only in Turkish. The Mayan Indians of Guatemala are placed in villages where they must speak Spanish rather than their own languages. In Australia many Aboriginal people lost their languages after white settlers invaded their lands. In Wales, the Welsh language is now taught alongside English, but less than a century ago, children who spoke Welsh in class were punished by their teachers.

If their mother tongue is treated as inferior, children may feel stupid or frightened, or ashamed of their language and culture. Gaining respect for your mother tongue is not just important for freedom of expression but is part of a greater struggle for human rights, for equality of treatment and for political rights. This is Nicole's story:

'We Kanaks are a Melanesian people. We have lived in these beautiful islands for thousands of years, cultivating yams and fruits, and fishing in the rivers and sea. Everyone belonged to a tribe and each tribe had its own land, languages and culture.

'In the nineteenth century the French Government seized our islands and said that they belonged to France. For us Kanaks it was a disaster. We lost our fertile land. European diseases and alcohol killed many of our people, and others died fighting the French.

In New Caledonia most of the low-paid jobs are done by the Kanaks, or people from other Pacific islands.

Many French people settled here, and that is why today we Kanaks are a minority in our own land.

'The Kanaks were treated as second-class citizens. The French settlers had the best houses, the best jobs, the best land. Kanaks protested against these injustices. They formed new political parties and demanded independence from France. There was fighting and some Kanaks died. In the end the French Government had to compromise. Kanaks have been given a much greater role in local government and we will all vote on independence in 1999.

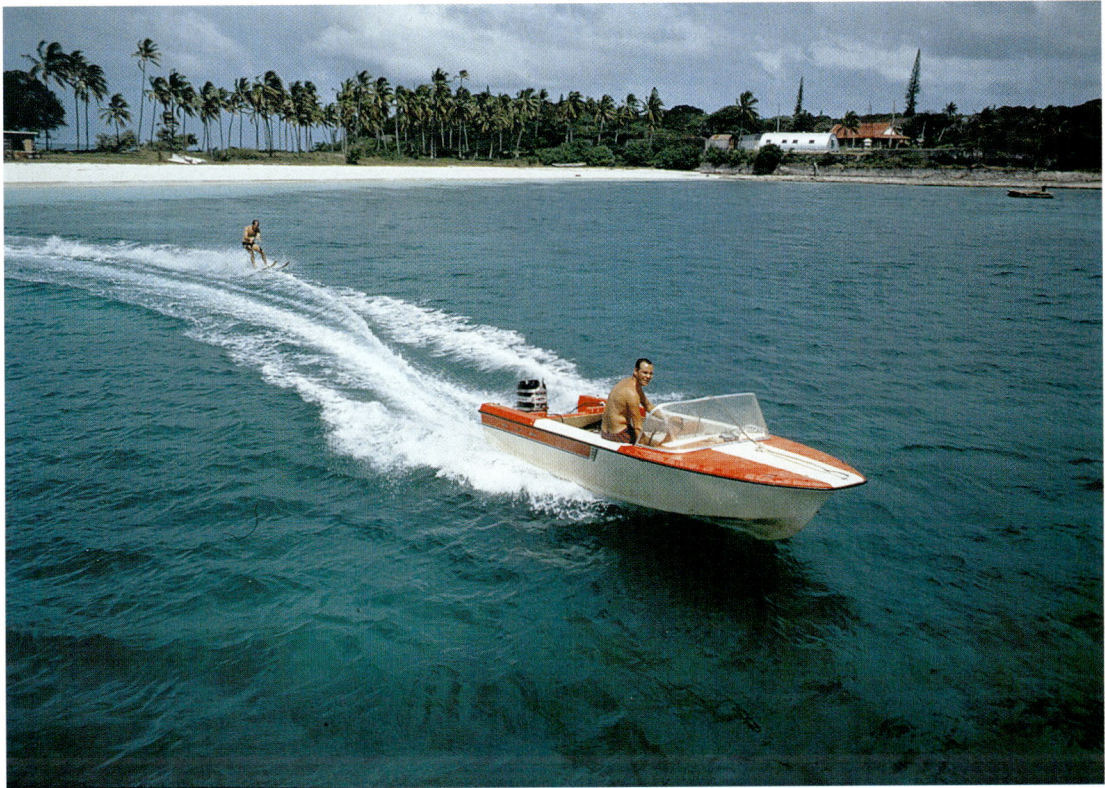

Many of the French people living in New Caledonia can afford a luxurious lifestyle, unlike most Kanaks.

'I became involved in the independence struggle through the alternative school movement. Let me explain. At home we speak our Melanesian language, but when I started primary school, suddenly I was expected to speak and think only in French. It was a huge shock. Everything we were taught in school was about France, especially how wonderful France was! Our own traditions and culture were ignored. It's not surprising that most Kanak children never finished primary school. I was one of the very few who graduated from high school and got a scholarship to study in France.

'I learnt a lot in France, not just about education but also about human rights and political ideas. When I returned to Kanaky in 1984 I was supposed to become a teacher myself, but I couldn't face teaching Kanak children all the same lies I had learnt myself. I felt that teaching in a foreign language was wrong and that young children should be educated in their own language, and learn about their culture and way of life.

Education is not just for young people but for everyone. Here Kanak women study posters supporting Kanak independence.

'In 1985 our independence movement decided that all children should stay away from school for one month as a protest against the education system. Most Kanak students joined in the boycott. But we knew that staying away from school wouldn't help these students in the long run, because when we gained independence we would need educated people. So we decided to found our own education system. We set up the *écoles populaires kanakes* (Kanak popular schools) – or EPK for short.

'First of all, we got together teachers, parents, students and our tribal elders and asked for their advice. Everyone said that our education system should teach Kanak children about Kanak traditions and culture, and also about practical things, like farming and fishing. Of course, we should learn subjects like maths, reading and writing, but these should be taught in our Melanesian languages. Children should learn French too, but only as a second language, after they had learnt their own language.

38

'Within a year the EPK movement had spread throughout Kanaky. We had 260 volunteer teachers and 1,500 students in forty-six schools. Of course, we also had enormous problems, because there were hardly any materials or trained teachers, and we had no official backing at all. At the same time we Kanaks were establishing our own newspaper called *Bwenando*, and our own radio, Radio Djiido. The French Government tried to stop us but we didn't give up.

'I worked with the EPK for many years. Some of the early enthusiasm disappeared and a few students returned to the French schools, but the ideas remained. When the French Government finally agreed that Kanaks must take a greater role in government and that Melanesian culture must be supported, we felt that some of our aims had been achieved. Now I am working with the Kanak Councils to bring our ideas to the official education system.'

This Kanak man is building a pirogue, a traditional dug-out canoe. For the Kanaks, independence means not just political freedom but also the recognition of their traditional skills and culture.

8
Words of hatred

As we have seen in previous chapters, many governments attempt to limit freedom of expression. We have tried to show how these limitations are not just a violation of an individual's basic human rights but are harmful to society as a whole.

In chapter 1, we also said that freedom of expression implies responsibilities and duties as well as rights. It should not mean freedom to lie or to spread hatred and violence. In fact, the same international law which upholds freedom of expression also gives situations where governments can restrict freedom of expression. The International Covenant on Civil and Political Rights lists four types of restrictions.

Firstly, governments may act to protect a person's legal rights and good name (such as from gossip or lies). Secondly, restrictions can be used for the protection of national security (as in wartime), or of public health (e.g., cigarette advertisements), or morals (e.g., pornography), or to prevent panic and chaos (such as after a disaster). As these categories are broad, the Covenant states that restrictions should be limited by law and used by governments only when absolutely necessary. If someone disagrees with the restrictions he or she should be free to state this and also to use the law to challenge the government.

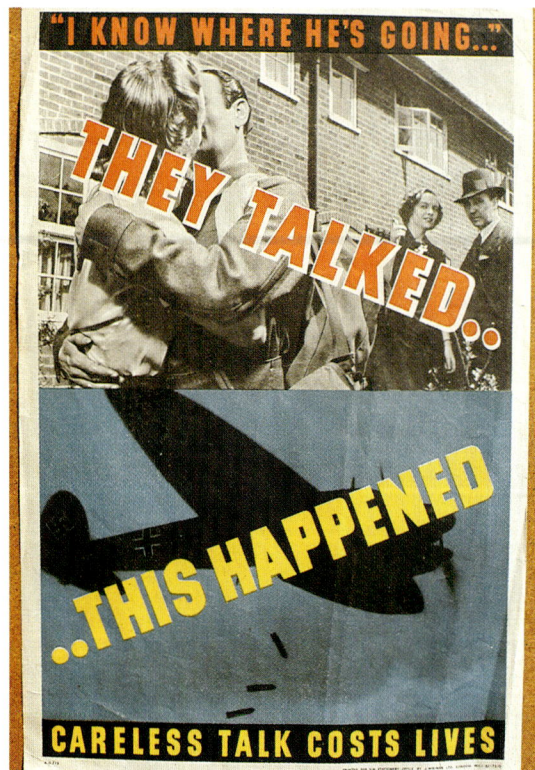

A British Second World War poster warning against 'loose talk' which might help the enemy.

The Covenant then lists two areas where restrictions are absolute. It says that governments must completely ban any propaganda for war and any material that encourages discrimination or violence against particular groups of people, such as ethnic minorities or religious believers. In effect, it is saying that there should be no freedom of expression for people who spread such ideas, because by doing so they are depriving others of their human rights. When there is a conflict between two sorts of rights – the right to freedom of expression and the right to life and security – then the right to life and security is the more important.

This might seem fairly straightforward but in reality it can be very complex. You may have heard the saying, 'Sticks and stones may break my bones, but words can never hurt me.' Is this true? Can some words hurt people so much that the words should be banned and those who use them be punished? How do we determine which words will lead to violence? Does it depend on certain circumstances, or apply only to some groups of people rather than others? Who is to decide which speech or writings are wrong, while others are permitted?

Germany is a country where the issue of freedom of expression is frequently discussed, because its people remember the past. When Adolf Hitler's National Socialist Party (the Nazi Party) came to power in 1933, it banned all the other political parties and took control of the press and radio.

This picture, taken in 1941, shows inmates of Sachsenhausen concentration camp in Germany. They were imprisoned by the Nazi government.

Neo-Nazis marching in modern Germany. Some neo-Nazis have killed and injured foreigners and burned down refugee hostels.

Any person who expressed criticism was arrested and taken to jail or to a concentration camp. Writers, artists and musicians could not work freely. The government conducted campaigns of hate against minority groups such as Jews, Roma (gypsies) and homosexuals. Later, as warring Germany occupied Europe, millions of these people were killed in concentration camps.

After Germany was defeated in 1945, it was occupied by the Allied forces. The Allies were determined that what had happened in Germany should never happen again. This was one of the main inspirations behind the foundation of the United Nations and the proclamation of the Universal Declaration of Human Rights. Most Germans were shocked and ashamed at what had been done in their name; there was a strong feeling that future German governments should act against any attempts to restore any aspect of the Nazi period.

Between 1948 and 1990 there were two German states. The Federal Republic of Germany (West Germany) gradually became a prosperous and democratic state, while the German

Democratic Republic (East Germany) was dominated by the USSR and had a Communist government. Both states declared that they totally opposed Nazism and would keep alive the memory of those who had suffered under it. In 1990 the two Germanies joined together to form one democratic state.

The creation of this new state has led to many new tensions. The level of unemployment in the eastern part of Germany rose rapidly after unification. Conflict in eastern Europe and in other parts of the world meant that hundreds of thousands of refugees fled to Germany. Some Germans, from both East and West, blamed these foreigners for their problems. Political groups following the Nazi ideas of Hitler (called neo-Nazis) became stronger, and their supporters started attacking foreigners and the hostels where refugees were staying. In 1992, more than 2,000 such attacks were recorded.

Jutta is a fourteen-year-old German girl who lives in Munich, southern Germany. Like many other Germans, she is deeply disturbed by neo-Nazism. Just before Christmas 1992 she joined over 350,000 other people in Munich in a candle-lit demonstration against racism. She says: 'We've learnt a lot at school about Germany's Nazi past but I used to think that it was just history, and that no one would want to bring Nazism back. But these neo-Nazis really want to do just that. They say that Hitler didn't really kill the Jews, that it was a lie made up by the Jews after the war, and they believe we should have Germany for the Germans and get rid of all the foreigners.

'My mother says that the best way to deal with neo-Nazis is to ban the lot of them. They talk about their right to freedom of expression but they are only interested in the freedom to beat, injure and kill. She says if they had banned the original Nazis from the beginning, then Hitler would never have come to power.

'My father doesn't agree. He says that if people commit acts of violence they should be punished severely. But he says most neo-Nazis are just pathetic – full of fiery talk. If we ban them, they'll just hide but they'll still be there. There really aren't very many of them, so why exaggerate their importance? Eventually people will tire of them and they will lose support.

'Our next-door neighbours originally came from East Germany. They say that under the former Communist government there was no freedom of expression at all, and everybody was afraid of the *Stasi* [secret police]. The main reason why some East Germans agree with the neo-Nazis is because they have never learnt how to think critically about political ideas. They say that if the government starts banning one group who knows where it will all end?

'I can't agree with any of these views. Perhaps the numbers of neo-Nazis are small, but they are growing fast. Look at the fear they are creating and the hatred they spread. Some of my Turkish classmates say that neo-Nazis have followed them, shouting at them to go back to Turkey. They paint rude and racist slogans near their houses and on their mosques. They say that it is only a matter of time before they are attacked.

'Personally, I think that the government should take very tough action against anyone who threatens violence, even if it is just by words. But in the end it's up to us to make sure that the neo-Nazis are stopped. We can't just ignore them and hope they will disappear. We have to keep educating people so they understand how important it is to stop them before they grow more powerful. I'll keep on talking and demonstrating. I'm sure most Germans don't want the past to return.'

Most Germans are deeply opposed to the neo-Nazis and millions have joined demonstrations against them. These young protesters in Berlin in 1990 are much more typical of young Germans today than are the neo-Nazis.

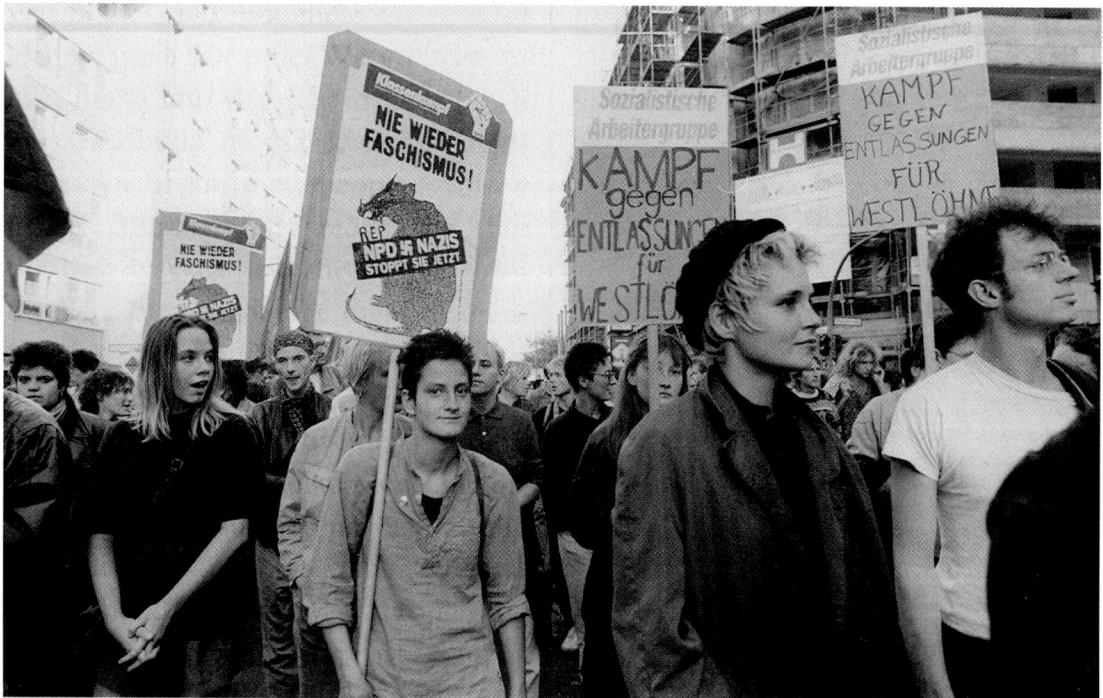

Glossary

Autobiography The story of a person's life, written by him or herself.

Boycott To protest by staying away from a place or not using a product.

Censor To remove material from books, magazines or other kinds of media because it is considered dangerous or unsuitable.

Concentration camp A guarded prison camp.

Democracy Rule by a government that is elected by the people.

Detain Imprison.

Dictatorship Government by a person or people who have not been elected and are not responsible to any legal system or other safeguards.

Discrimination Treating a certain group of people badly because of negative feelings about their skin colour, language, religion or political beliefs.

Ethnic minority A group of people who share a language, religion or culture which makes them feel different to the majority population.

Exile To send someone away from his or her country as a punishment.

Heritage A name, land, language, religion, culture or a combination of all of these, which can be handed down from one generation to another.

Homosexual A person whose sexual preference is for people of their own gender.

Indigenous peoples The first or original peoples of a land.

Intimidate To threaten, bully or scare someone.

Legal system An elaborate system of rules which lays down how individuals should behave towards each other, how governments should behave towards individuals and how individuals can join together in organizations.

Melanesia The area of the Western Pacific which includes Papua New Guinea, the Solomon Islands, Vanuatu and New Caledonia.

Political prisoner A person jailed because the government says that his or her political beliefs or actions are harmful.

Propaganda Information or ideas that persuade people to support or to oppose a government.

Refugee Someone who has fled a country because he or she is being persecuted by the government.

Repeal To reverse a law.

State A nation with borders and a government, which is recognized by other states.

United Nations (UN) An organization, formed in 1945, which has almost all the states of the world as members. It aims to keep world peace, promote human rights and support development.

Violation The disregarding of a right, or the breaking of a law or agreement.

Further reading

The recommended reading age appears after each entry.

General books on human rights

Human Rights Activity File by Graham Pike and David Sherwin (Stanley Thomas, Cheltenham, 1990). 11–18

New Rights for Children (Save the Children/ UNICEF, 1990). Learning materials and teachers' handbook on the Convention on the Rights of the Child. 9–14

Working for Freedom: A Human Rights Education Pack (Amnesty International, 1991). A classroom resource with a section on imprisoned writers. Available from AI British Section. 11–18

Books on freedom of expression

Censorship by Christian Wolmar (Wayland, 1990). Presents arguments for and against censorship. 12–18

Free Expressions: Amnesty International Art Education Pack by Sara Selwood (Amnesty International, 1991). Teachers' workbook with case studies demonstrating links between art and human rights. Available from AI British Section. 14–19

'First they came for the Jews': the legacy of Pastor Niemoeller (Minority Rights Group Education Pack, 1991). 11+

Freedom of Expression and Minorities under Nazism Available from MRG. 11+

Freedom of Expression in the United Kingdom (Liberty Briefing no. 14, 1989). 16+

Let's Discuss Disability by Ruth Bailey (Wayland, 1989). Chapter on communication among disabled people. 11–14

Fiction and biography

Animal Farm by George Orwell (Penguin, 1945). The classic story of a revolution that goes wrong. 11+

The Day They Came to Arrest the Book by Nat Hentoff (Penguin Books, 1988). A story about a high school that tries to ban *Huckleberry Finn*. 13–18

Fahrenheit 451 by Ray Bradbury (Corgi, 1954). Story of a society that burns books and of those who fight to save them. 14+

I Rigoberta, The Story of an Indian Woman from Guatemala; this is *'I, Rigoberta Menchu': The Story of an Indian Woman from Guatemala*, adapted for young readers, 1992. (Available with Teachers' Pack and slide set from Central American Human Rights Committee, 83 Margaret St, London W1N 7HB). 9–14

The Wave by Morton Rhue (Penguin, 1988). A thriller about the rise of fanaticism in a US high school history class. 13–18

Useful addresses

Amnesty International (AI) works with prisoners of conscience. Article 19 works for freedom of expression. P.E.N. helps imprisoned writers and artists.

Australia

Amnesty International
Australian Section
Private Bag 23, Broadway
Sydney, 2007

Melbourne P.E.N. Centre
PO Box 143, Cliffon Hill
Victoria, 3068

NSW Council for Civil
Liberties
PO Box 201, Glebe
NSW, 2037

Sydney P.E.N. Centre
PO Box 153
Woollahra, NSW, 2025

Britain & N. Ireland

Amnesty International –
British Section
99–119 Rosebury Ave
London EC1R 4RE

Article 19
90 Borough High St
London SE1 1LL

English Centre of P.E.N.
7 Dilke St
London SW3 4JE

Index on Censorship
32 Queen Victoria St
London EC4N 4SS

Liberty/Civil Liberties Trust
21 Tabard St
London SE1 4LA

Minority Rights Group
379 Brixton Rd
London SW9 7DE

Northern Ireland Civil
Liberties Council
45/7 Donegall St
Belfast, BT1 2FG

Scottish Council for Civil
Liberties
146 Holland St
Glasgow G2 4NG

Canada

Amnesty International
Canadian section
(English–speaking)
130 Slater St, Suite 900
Ottawa, Ontario, K1P 6E2

Amnistie Internationale
Section Canadienne
(French–speaking)
6250 Boulevard Monk
Montreal, Quebec, H4E 3H7

Article 19, Canada
PO Box 489 Cannington
Ontario L0E 1EW

Canadian Committee to
Protect Journalists
490 Adelaide St.West,
Suite 205
Toronto, Ontario M5V 1T2

Canadian P.E.N. Centre
24 Ryerson Ave
Toronto, Ontario, M5T 2P3

Canadian Rights and
Liberties Federation
323 Chapel St
Ottawa, Ontario, K1N 7Z2

Centre quebecois du P.E.N.
615 rue belmont
Montreal, Quebec, H3B 2L8

Republic of Ireland

Amnesty International
Sean McBride House
8 Shaw St, Dublin 2

Irish Council for Civil
Liberties
c/o 18 Villiers Rd, Dublin 6

New Zealand

Amnesty International
New Zealand Section
PO Box 793
Wellington

New Zealand Council for
Civil Liberties
PO Box 337
Wellington

New Zealand P.E.N. Centre
P0 Box 34 – 631
Birkenhead, Auckland 10

USA

American Civil Liberties
Union
132 West 43rd St
New York, NY 10036

American P.E.N. Center
568 Broadway, 4th Floor
New York, NY, 10012

Amnesty International of the
USA
322 Eighth Ave
New York, NY 10001

Committee to Protect
Journalists
16 East 42nd St, Third Floor
New York, NY 10017

Fund for Free
Expression/Article 19
485 Fifth Ave
New York, NY 10017

National Emergency Civil
Liberties Committee
175 Fifth Ave
New York, NY 10010

P.E.N. Center USA West
672 South Lafayette Park Pl,
Suite 41
Los Angeles, CA 90057

Index

Words printed in **bold** indicate subjects shown in pictures.